relationships

Participant's Guide

Resources by Les and Leslie Parrott

Books

Becoming Soul Mates
Getting Ready for the Wedding
Like a Kiss on the Lips
Love Is
The Marriage Mentor Manual
Questions Couples Ask
Relationships
Relationships Workbook
Saving Your Marriage Before It Starts
Saving Your Marriage Before It Starts Workbook for Men
Saving Your Marriage Before It Starts Workbook for Women

Video Curriculum

Saving Your Marriage Before It Starts
Mentoring Engaged and Newlywed Couples

Audio Pages

Relationships
Saving Your Marriage Before It Starts

Website

www.realrelationships.com

relationships

An Open and Honest Guide to Making Bad Relationships
Better and Good Relationships Great

Participant's Guide

Drs. Les and Leslie Parrott
with Sharon E. Lamson

ZondervanPublishingHouse
Grand Rapids, Michigan

A Division of HarperCollinsPublishers

Relationships Participant's Guide
Copyright © 1999 by Les and Leslie Parrott

Requests for information should be addressed to:

🏭 ZondervanPublishingHouse
Grand Rapids, Michigan 49530

ISBN 0-310-22585-X

Interior design by Sherri Hoffman

Printed in the United States of America

02 03 04 05 / ❖ DC/ 10 9 8 7 6 5 4 3 2

contents

introduction

Relationships—all of us have or have had special relationships in our lives. When we were young, we had a relationship with our parents or caregivers. As we grew, we developed relationships with children in our neighborhood and school. As teenagers we discovered relationships with the opposite sex. And as adults, we add relationships with coworkers, fellow committee members, clients, and others.

This course is an enhancement tool. If you struggle with relationships, these six sessions can help you smooth out some of the rough edges. If you already enjoy good relationships, this course can serve as a guide to making them even better.

This course is based on the book *Relationships* by Drs. Les and Leslie Parrott. Each session is about fifty minutes long and includes the following elements:

Overview. Lets you know up front what the goals for the session are.

Video Clips. Intermingles illustrative vignettes with clips of Les and Leslie talking about pertinent topics.

Conference Call. Large-group discussion.

Huddle Time. Small-group discussion of about three or four people.

On Your Own. Independent exercises to help you evaluate yourself.

Extra-Mile Exercises. Optional outside-the-classroom activities. These exercises won't be discussed during class time but will serve to help you dig deeper into the material covered.

Session Summary. A quick review of the main points of the session.

Closing Prayer.

By the time you come to the end of this course, we believe you will have the tools you need to develop strong relationships. We wish you every comfort and blessing healthy relationships bring, and we pray you will never take them for granted.

Les and Leslie Parrott
Seattle, Washington

the compulsion for completion

Overview

In this session you will

- investigate your relational readiness.
- uncover two lies that sabotage relationships.
- take a look at the masks you wear in various settings and discuss ways to discard the unhealthy ones.
- explore four steps you can take toward becoming whole.

Video:
The Compulsion for Completion

The Importance of Wholeness

Anne's Behavior

Two Lies That Sabotage Relationships

Four Components of Becoming Whole

Conference Call:
Two Lies That Sabotage Relationships

Sociologist George Herbert Mead once said, "The _____ can only exist in _____ to other selves."

Lie Number One

I _____ this person to be _____.

Lie Number Two

If this person needs _____, I will be _____.

Conference Call:
Four Steps to Becoming Whole

If you try to find _____ with another person
before achieving a sense of _____ on your own, all your relationships become an attempt to _____
_____.

    People who become whole learn to
    heal their _____.
    remove their _____.
    sit in the _____.
    rely on _____.

On Your Own:
Relational Readiness

To help you assess how ready you are to engage in friendships and other meaningful relationships, respond to each item listed below using the following scale:

4—Often
3—Sometimes
2—Seldom
1—Never

____ I feel a sense of relief when I don't have to be alone.

____ Any relationship is better than no relationship at all.

____ I experience a little bit of panic when I think of not having someone to be close to.

____ The very idea of solitude strikes fear in my heart.

____ I'm tempted to settle for any kind of friendship because I'm not sure I'll find just the right friend for me.

____ In most of my relationships, I wait to be "selected" rather than taking the initiative myself to do the selecting.

____ When I have special friendships, I feel better about myself.

____ I don't like to be alone.

____ I don't have a very clear idea of the personal qualities I look for in a person in terms of friendship.

____ If I don't have someone to be close to, I feel less complete.

Scoring: Add the numbers you have placed next to each statement. There is a possible total of forty points. To interpret your score, use the following scale:

30–40 There is a strong indication that you have a need to establish a healthier sense of your identity and personal wholeness. You will want to pay special attention to the four steps toward wholeness discussed in the video.

20–29 You have done some significant work in establishing a healthy identity and a good sense of self-worth. There's still work to do, however, in continuing to construct an integrated and whole sense of self that will help to ensure healthier relationships.

1–19 You have an established sense of security in who you are and a confident perspective on your sense of personal wholeness, which should serve you well in your relationships.

On Your Own:
Taking Off Your Masks

This exercise will help you become more aware of the masks you sometimes use to guard against feeling judged or negatively evaluated. It focuses on three areas: work, home, and church. Feel free to add other areas, as well.

I wear masks at work (or school):

Very Often   *Almost Never*

1   2   3   4   5   6   7

If your answer was between one and four, describe the kinds of masks you wear and with whom.

_____

_____

_____

I wear masks at home:

Very Often   *Almost Never*

1   2   3   4   5   6   7

If your answer was between one and four, describe the kinds of masks you wear and with whom.

_____

_____

_____

I wear masks at church:

Very Often   *Almost Never*

| 1 | 2 | 3 | 4 | 5 | 6 | 7 |

If your answer was between one and four, describe the kinds of masks you wear and with whom.

_____

_____

_____

_____

Huddle Time:
Masks We Wear

- How willing and comfortable are you in disclosing yourself to others and letting yourself be known by others?

- What social masks do you sometimes wear that guard your vulnerability?

- What can you do to discard unhealthy masks? Are all masks unhealthy?

Extra-Mile Exercise

Getting into the "driver's seat"—especially when you've lived most of your life as a passenger—will take hard work, initiative, purpose, and clear-cut goals. Healthy relationships will grow out of your having an identity, a purpose, courage, and commitment.

The following exercise will help you construct a personal statement of purpose and then create goals to help you fulfill that purpose. Begin by determining what you value. Though difficult, force yourself to rank the following twelve values with "1" being the most important to you.

_____ **Achievement**—feeling satisfaction from a job well done.

_____ **Challenges**—using creativity, training, and intelligence to overcome obstacles.

_____ **Education**—increasing your intellectual understanding of life.

_____ **Aesthetics**—appreciating the beauty in people, art, or nature.

_____ **Health**—feeling good in a physical and emotional sense.

_____ **Independence**—having the freedom to do your own thing.

_____ **Morality**—maintaining your moral, ethical, and religious standards.

_____ **Pleasure**—having time to play and have a good time.

_____ **Relationships**—caring for, sharing with, and giving to those close to you.

_____ **Spirituality**—cultivating a meaningful and personal relationship with God.

_____ **Security**—feeling safe; free from unexpected and unpleasant changes.

_____ **Service to Others**—knowing you have benefited others.

_____ **Wealth**—improving your financial position.

Ponder the values that are most meaningful to you. Consider how your top three or four values can be incorporated into a meaningful statement of purpose. This statement does not need to be permanent, as it will change throughout your life. For now, draft something that seems right for you at this time in your life—something that is personally compelling and comes from the heart.

My purpose:

_____

_____

_____

Now that your purpose statement has been drafted, note some specific and obtainable goals that will serve as a means to fulfill it.

Short-term goals (obtainable within the next three or four months)

1. _____

_____

2. _____

_____

3. _____

_____

Long-term goals (obtainable within the next year or more)

1. _____

_____

2. _____

_____

3. _____

_____

Specifically, what immediate gratifications will you have to delay in order to achieve your goals?

_____

_____

_____

_____

Example

Statement of Purpose:
 To follow God's leading as I establish my career and grow in my involvement in my church.

Short-Term Goals:
 1. Seek God's will through prayer, Bible reading, and journaling.
 2. Meet with my supervisor to establish my career path.
 3. Take a computer class to improve skills.
 4. Meet with my pastor to discuss where I could minister in the church.

Long-Term Goals:
 1. To be promoted within a year.
 2. To be in charge of a ministry at church.

Delayed Gratification:
 1. Get up earlier so as to spend daily time with God.
 2. Drop chamber choir so I can take on a church ministry.
 3. Save $50 a month in order to pay for computer class.

Session Two

keeping family ties from
pulling strings

Overview

In this session you will

- review the lessons you've learned at home.
- reflect on the "unspoken rules."
- discuss how childhood lessons and rules affect our present-day relationships.

Video:
Keeping Family Ties
from Pulling Strings

The Most Powerful Emotional System We Belong To

Frank and Lily's Relationship

The Three Rs

Family Rules

Family Roles

Family Relationships

On Your Own:
How Healthy Is Your Home?

How we relate to members of our own family and how they relate to us sets the pattern for how we will relate to all other relationships. While no family is perfect, some are healthier than others. In her book *Traits of a Healthy Family*, Dolores Curran reveals the top fifteen healthy traits as repeatedly noted by family experts. They are listed below.

Using the following scale, rate the degree to which your family of origin is or was characterized by these desirable traits. (You may want to take this survey again, rating your present family situation, if applicable.)

4—Much of the time
3—Some of the time
2—Rarely
1—Almost never

Family of Origin		*Current Family*
____	Communicates and listens.	____
____	Affirms and supports one another.	____
____	Teaches respect for others.	____
____	Develops a sense of trust.	____
____	Has a sense of play and humor.	____
____	Exhibits a sense of shared responsibility.	____
____	Teaches a sense of right and wrong.	____
____	Has a strong sense of family in which rituals and traditions abound.	____
____	Has a balance of interaction among members.	____
____	Has a shared religious core.	____
____	Respects the privacy of one another.	____

_____ Values service to others.   _____
_____ Fosters family table time and conversation.   _____
_____ Shares leisure time.   _____
_____ Admits to and seeks help with problems.   _____
_____ **Total**   _____

Scoring: Add the numbers you have placed beside each item. There is a possible total of sixty points. To interpret your score, use the following:

50–60:   Count your blessings. You grew up in a relatively loving home free of dysfunction. Your caregivers took time to nurture your development and cultivate an atmosphere that was positive and caring. Your relationships will certainly benefit from this good foundation.

30–49:   Your family health falls into the midrange, or average zone. Your family of origin may not be all you would have liked it to be, but then again, things could have been a lot worse. Learn from the tensions and disengaged style that was present in your home. How did you contribute to it? What could you have done to make things better? In your present family situation, do you contribute to the tension? How? In what ways can you make things better now?

1–29:   Unfortunately, this range is where you find families with the most strife. Perhaps you have experienced a lot of distressed and polarized relationships (even abusive ones) at home. If so, this will present some challenges to your present and future relationships, but nothing that can't be overcome with learning good relational skills.

Huddle Time:
Our Family of Origin

- In what ways has your family of origin shaped your personality, your career choice, your relationships, and your values?

- In what specific ways does your family still "pull your strings"? In other words, how do your early family influences still manifest themselves in your present relationships?

Conference Call: The Three Rs

Family rules unconsciously guide individuals by describing what family members should do and how they should behave, even if they fly in the face of a person's real desires.

The three Rs every family teaches are:

R _ules_

R _ales_

R _isponsibilities_

Samples of Unspoken Rules

- Don't reveal your _feelings_.
- Never hide your _____.
- Always get your _____.
- Never raise your _____.
- Do everything you can to _____.
- _____ whenever you can.
- _Trust_ others only after they've earned it.
- Never call _attention_ to yourself.
- Let others know your _____.
- Put on a _____.
- Always be _____.

Typical Roles Played Out in a Family

- _____: Always ready with a solution
- _____: Pulling compassion and sympathy from others.
- _____: Diving into situations for somebody else's safety.
- _____: Ready with a joke for comic relief.

- _____: Serving as a bridge between others.
- _____: Facing reality and calling it as you see it.
- _____: Administering healing to emotional wounds.
- _____: Holding a confidence tight and safe.

On Your Own:
Lessons Learned from Mom and Dad

The following exercise will help you evaluate how each of your parents (or primary caregivers) behaved. Take about ten minutes to rate their effectiveness on a scale of one to ten, with one being the least effective. As time allows, write a brief description of how each person performed each skill.

Category	Mother	Father
Talking about his/her experiences	____	____
Showing his/her feelings	____	____
Standing up for himself/herself	____	____
Being a good listener	____	____
Understanding others' perspectives	____	____
Managing anger	____	____
Accepting responsibility (not passing the buck)	____	____
Working for equitable solutions	____	____

Huddle Time:
How Our Families Have Influenced Our Relationships

- In what ways has your family of origin influenced the relationships you have with other people today?

- Of the three major ways families shape us—rules, roles, and relationships—which one do you see as the most influential for you and why?

Extra-Mile Exercise

What were the unspoken rules in your family of origin? The following exercise will help you pinpoint some of the rules you may have absorbed. Complete the following sentence stems with whatever first pops into your mind.

Men should _____

_____

Women should _____

_____

Success is _____

_____

The most important thing is _____

_____

Life _____

_____

Now review what you have written and edit it to conform to how you believe your parents would have completed these sentences. This will give you a pretty good start at uncovering your family's unspoken rules. Use the space below to write any additional rules that may not have been articulated but were still known.

_____

_____

_____

_____

In what specific ways do your family's unspoken rules influence your relationships?

_____

_____

_____

_____

Session Three

crossing the gender line

Overview

In this session you will

- discover gender differences.
- examine what women need to know about men.
- explore what men need to know about women.
- discuss what it would be like to be the opposite sex.

Video:
Crossing the Gender Line

Leslie's Story about Winnie the Pooh and Piglet

Anne and Tom in the Gym

Men Tend to Be

Women Tend to Be

Importance of Simple Communication and Sharing

Conference Call:
Exploring Our Gender Roles

- Consider your cross-gender relationships. What aspects of these relationships with the opposite sex (excluding romantic relationships) seem to be easier than relationships with the same sex?

- When you were growing up, what social activities or games influenced your perception of gender roles?

On Your Own:
What's Your Gender IQ?

How much do you know about the fundamental differences between men and women? Label the following statements as either true or false to find out how much you already know.

T   F   Women are better spellers than men.

T   F   Men are more likely than women to use conversation to solve problems.

T   F   Women have larger connections between their brain's left and right hemispheres.

T   F   Men are better at reading the emotions of others than women are.

T   F   Men score higher on the math section of the SAT than do women.

T   F   In comparison to men, women are better at maintaining a sense of geographical location.

T   F   Men are better than women at fitting suitcases into a crowded car trunk.

T   F   Women are better than men at describing their feelings.

T   F   Men, more than women, focus their energy on achievement.

T   F   Women, more than men, give priority to relationships.

Scoring: Each of these statements are based on current gender research studies. The correct answers are: 1-T, 2-T, 3-T, 4-F, 5-T, 6-F, 7-T, 8-T, 9-T, 10-T. The more items you answered correctly, the better your knowledge of gender differences.

On Your Own:
What If You Were the Opposite Sex?

Take fifteen minutes to put yourself into the shoes of the opposite sex. If you are a man, imagine what it would be like for you to be a woman. If you are a woman, how would being a man change your perspective? Be as honest as you can as you answer the following questions.

1. What is your first reaction to living as the opposite sex?

    _____

    _____

    _____

    _____

2. How would the simple task of getting ready in the morning be different if you were the opposite gender? Take into consideration the time it would take, what you would do, how you would dress.

    _____

    _____

    _____

    _____

3. How would living as the opposite sex affect your career choice and other aspirations?

    _____

    _____

    _____

    _____

4. As the opposite gender, would you feel more or less safe in society? Why?

     _____

     _____

     _____

     _____

5. Would you feel any different about marriage or relationships with the opposite sex if you were the opposite gender? If so, how?

     _____

     _____

     _____

     _____

6. How would your relationship with both your parents differ if you were the opposite gender?

     _____

     _____

     _____

     _____

Share your responses in your small-group discussion.

Extra-Mile Exercise

Do some more self-examination. If possible, share your responses with your spouse or a close friend.

1. Describe your experience of completing the exercises for this session. What did you learn about yourself?

   _____

   _____

   _____

2. This session noted several things men and women should know about each other. What differences can you add?

   _____

   _____

   _____

3. Women use their conversation to build "rapport," while men use conversation to give or get a "report." Cite examples from your own experience that support this statement.

   _____

   _____

   _____

4. We doom relationships with the opposite sex when we try to change them into becoming more like us. What can you do to accept and even appreciate the different qualities of the other gender?

   _____

   _____

   _____

   _____

Session Four

friends to die for

Overview

In this session you will

- investigate what friends are for.
- determine what are the right kinds of friends.
- discover how good friends are made.
- discuss the qualities that comprise a good friendship.

Video:
Friends to Die For

Friendship Actually Cures Stress

Friends of the Road

Friends of the Heart

Lily and Bette Working It Out

Qualities That Make a Great Friend

On Your Own:
The Friendship Assessment

This exercise will help you evaluate the current condition of each of your friendships. Take ten minutes to evaluate one to three friendships. You can always go back and evaluate other friendships on your own. Read each statement and determine if it is true or false for each friend you are evaluating.

Answer T or F

Friend #1	Friend #2	Friend #3	Characteristics
___	___	___	This person knows how to keep a secret.
___	___	___	We can disagree and then make up without holding grudges.
___	___	___	This person almost always makes time for me, and I do the same for him/her.
___	___	___	When he/she gives me advice, it is generally without judgment.
___	___	___	I can totally be myself around this person.
___	___	___	He/she is a good listener.
___	___	___	This person has stuck by me through tough times and is willing to make personal sacrifices for me.
___	___	___	This person knows my faults but loves me anyway.
___	___	___	Our relationship is balanced with give and take; we are equally vulnerable and caring.
___	___	___	I am able to set clear boundaries with this person when necessary, and he/she respects them.
___	___	___	No subject is off-limits in our conversation.

___   ___   ___   I can always count on this person.

___   ___   ___   **Total Number of T Responses**

Scoring: Add up the number of true responses for each friendship you evaluated. There is a possible total of twelve points for each relationship. Interpret your score using the following:

10–12 No doubt about it, this is a good friend who is worth all the effort, care, and investigation. You will want to do all that you can to nurture this relationship and enjoy it.

7–9   Though this person could be more sensitive to your needs, this friend shows great potential. Be careful, however, not to set yourself up for disappointment if this person doesn't meet all your expectations.

0–6   This friend is probably too fair-weather to see you through stormy times (and maybe even the sunny ones too). Don't hang all your hopes on this one.

On Your Own:
Are You a "Growth-Promoting" Listener?

Friendship is a long _____.

Indeed, the ability to generate good talk by the hour is the most promising indication, during the uncertain early stages, that a possible friendship will take hold.

There are two skills needed in carrying on a good conversation. The first one is the ability to _____. The second one is _____.

This second exercise assesses your strengths and areas for growth when it comes to the important friendship skill of listening. It is important that you be honest in answering each of the following three items.

1. Generally speaking, in meeting someone for the first time, are you *genuinely* interested in getting to know that person and understanding his/her story? Do you really want to know what interests that person? Or are you more likely to just go through the motions, being socially appropriate but not very genuine?

   Not Genuine   *Extremely Genuine*

   1   2   3   4   5   6   7

2. Generally speaking, in meeting someone for the first time, are you *accepting* of that person's opinions and feelings? Do you feel open to hearing what he or she has to say, or are you more likely to interject your opinions and feelings before completely understanding the other person's?

   Not Genuine   *Extremely Genuine*

   1   2   3   4   5   6   7

3. Generally speaking, in meeting someone for the first time, are you *empathic* with him or her? Do you put yourself in the other person's shoes and try to accurately understand his or her experience, or are you more likely to jump to a few conclusions and make a few assumptions?

Not Genuine   *Extremely Genuine*

1   2   3   4   5   6   7

_____Total Score

Scoring: Add up the numbers you have circled. There is a total of twenty-one points possible. The higher your score, the more likely you are to be a growth-promoting listener. However, you may find it more helpful to consider each continuum separately to see which of the three important qualities you will want to work on most.

Huddle Time:
Assessing Friendships

- It has been said that many people audition to be our friends but only a few make the cut. What is it about your friends that helped them "get the part"?

- Did it have more to do with circumstances or personal attributes?

- What were the circumstances or personal attributes?

Conference Call:
The Top Quality in a Friendship

Let's take a look at four qualities that are essential to any friendship:

- The quality that tops the list in survey after survey of what people appreciate most about their friends is _____.
- Every friend you'll ever have will eventually disappoint you. Count on it. That doesn't mean that every offense of a friend requires _____; some slights need only be overlooked and forgotten.
- _____ is not only expressed in words; it means being authentic. True friends aren't afraid to be honest, and they aren't afraid to be themselves.
- The meaning of _____ refers to the ability of two people to influence each other's plans, thoughts, actions, and emotions. Personal sacrifice. Selfless devotion. Commitment. These are the noble qualities dedication requires.
- Of the four qualities mentioned in the video, which is the most important one for you, and why?

Extra-Mile Exercise

This exercise will help you evaluate what kind of a friend *you* are. Consider what your friends would say about you when it comes to the following statements. Answer yes or no to each of these items as honestly as you can.

My friends would say ...

Y   N   I always keep my promises.
Y   N   I always stick up for them.
Y   N   I give them grace when they let me down.
Y   N   I am just as likely to genuinely celebrate my friends' successes as I am to comfort them in their disappointments.
Y   N   I am there when they need me.
Y   N   I never gossip about them or talk behind their back.
Y   N   I give them the benefit of the doubt.
Y   N   I hear them out even when I disagree.
Y   N   I stand by them through thick and thin.

Scoring: The more items you honestly responded to with a yes, the more likely you are to be loyal to your friends. If you answered yes to nearly all of the items, however, you probably shouldn't take this quality in yourself for granted. Check in with your friends. Ask them to give you a loyalty checkup by inviting them to give honest feedback on how you are doing with being loyal.

On the other hand, if you did not answer yes to very many of these items, you may want to talk to your friends about how you can better cultivate this quality. Remember, loyalty is what tops the list of what people appreciate most about their friends, so this is one you will want to spend some time on.

what to do when friends fail

Overview

In this session you will

- explore how much you can expect from a friend.
- examine why and how friends fail.
- look at five steps to take toward reconciliation.

Video:
What to Do When Friends Fail

Anne's Phone Conversation with Mark

Why Friends Fail: Change, Neglect, Betrayal

Five Steps to Reclaiming a Friendship

- Count the cost.
- Make meaningful contact.
- Forgive as best you can.
- Diagnose the problem.
- Rebuild respect.

On Your Own:
What You Expect from Friends

This exercise will help you clarify what you expect from your closest friends. Answer the following true-or-false statements as honestly as you can.

T   F   I expect my friend to know my faults but accept me anyway.

T   F   I expect my friend to never break special plans with me.

T   F   I expect my close friends to always keep their word on both big and small issues.

T   F   A really good friend should know how I'm feeling most of the time.

T   F   I expect my friend to say "I'm sorry" when he or she is wrong.

T   F   My closest friend should confide in me more than anyone else.

T   F   I expect my friend to always keep a secret.

T   F   It is difficult for me to forgive a friend who has hurt me in some way.

T   F   If we are truly friends, we should hardly ever have much conflict.

T   F   I expect my friends to never talk behind my back or break a confidence—even about small things.

T   F   My very closest friend should have no other friendships closer than ours.

T   F   If a good friend breaks a confidence or fails me in some other way, I am unlikely to give him or her a second or third chance.

T   F   I expect my friend to never hold a grudge against me.

T   F   I expect my friend to always admit when he or she is wrong.

   If you answered true to any of these items, you are more likely to have very high standards about how your friends should treat you. The more times you answered true, the more you expect from your friends and perhaps the more rigid you are with your expectations.

Conference Call:
Why Do Some Friends Fail?

- Why do friends fail?

- What friendships have failed for you? What happened? What were your expectations for these friendships?

On Your Own:
Learning from Your Own
Failed Friendships

This exercise is designed to help you gain insight into how you can avoid repeating patterns of painful relationships. Consider a relationship where a person you trusted failed you in some way, and answer the following questions to help you learn from the failure.

1. How long did you know this person, and what brought you together?

    _____

    _____

2. Looking back over your relationship, what kinds of things helped you to believe you could trust him or her?

    _____

    _____

3. In specific terms, what did this person do to "fail" you?

    _____

    _____

4. What percentage of the hurt was due to the following:

    Percentage
    _____ miscommunication
    _____ broken confidence
    _____ gossip
    _____ neglect
    _____ betrayal
    _____ uncontrollable change (moving away)
    _____ personality change
    _____ moral choices
    _____ other _____

5. Do some serious soul-searching and try to assess how much you were responsible for the falling-out with this friend. Was there anything you did or didn't do that may have contributed to the problem? If so, what was it?

_____

_____

_____

6. Did you ever want to get revenge as a result of the hurt you felt from this relationship? If so, why? Also, what did you do with your vengeful feelings, and what was the result?

_____

_____

_____

7. Have you come to a place of healing with the hurt you experienced? If so, what helped bring this about?

_____

_____

_____

_____

_____

8. In reviewing the basis for your relationship and the reasons for your falling-out, what can you surmise about how to avoid a similar situation in future friendships?

_____

_____

_____

_____

_____

Huddle Time:
The Hurt Involved in
Failed Friendships

- What caused the most hurt for you in a failed relationship you experienced?

- In what ways have you overcome the hurt you felt? Have you resolved those hurt feelings?

Conference Call:
Five Steps in Restoring Failed
Relationships

There are five steps to take in restoring a broken relationship:

- *Step One: Count the cost.* _____ whether your fractured friendship should be _____.
- *Step Two: Make meaningful contact.* Keep the message _____. Convey your desire to resolve your differences and explore their openness to considering a _____.
- *Step Three: Forgive as best you can.* Our primal urge for _____ comes to a screeching halt when we set our _____ aside and begin to _____.
- *Step Four: Diagnose the problem.* Acknowledge the _____. Realize that everyone is partially _____ and partially _____.
- *Step Five: Rebuild respect.* Begin by noting your friend's most _____. Next, own up to your mistakes. Offer a _____.

Of all the steps listed above, which one do you think would be the most difficult to take? What stumbling blocks might get in the way of making meaningful contact, forgiving the other person, diagnosing the problem, or even rebuilding respect?

Extra-Mile Exercise

Making amends can be the most difficult task in any relationship. Often there is a battle between our head and our heart. Our head wants to stay angry, to recount the wrongs we've endured; but our heart yearns to recapture the joy we once felt with that friend. Consider following these guidelines to help you bring healing and restoration to a floundering relationship.

Step One: Count the Cost

What is the price you are paying to keep this friendship alive? If you were forced to choose between the following two statements, which one would best describe how you feel about this relationship?

1. This relationship has redeeming qualities I value, and it is worth the cost of repairing and maintaining.
2. This relationship is unhealthy and forces me to compromise my convictions.

If you chose the second statement, it is time to make a clean break. If you chose the first statement, you are ready to make amends by progressing to the next step.

Step Two: Make Meaningful Contact

What will be the best way for you to let your friend know that the friendship is valuable to you and that you want to restore it? Knowing your friend, should you initiate contact through a brief note, a phone call, or a visit?

Once you determine the means, take care to send the right message by cleaning your heart and mind of lingering desires to get back at your friend. Take a moment right now to note what has hurt you and how you may still want to get even. Be honest with yourself about your anger and feelings of revenge.

_____

_____

_____

_____

Step Three: Forgive as Best You Can

Once you have a handle on your hurt and angry feelings, you will need to do your best to step beyond them by trying to forgive. While not easy, it is vital if you are going to make amends. Put yourself in your friend's shoes and try to see the relationship and situation from his or her perspective.

1. How do you imagine your friend feels about what is going on between the two of you?

    _____

    _____

2. Is your friend feeling as hurt as you are? If you think so, why?

    _____

    _____

3. If the roles were reversed, how do you think the relationship would be different?

    _____

    _____

4. Knowing that hardly any relationship problem is ever entirely one person's fault, what responsibility do you take for this situation?

    _____

    _____

5. Are you able and willing to set aside your pride and give grace to your friend? If so, how can you do this?

    _____

    _____

Step Four: Diagnose the Problem

Once you have come to a place where you can forgive your friend and convey the simple message of wanting to make things right, the two of you may need to explore together why the problem emerged so that it won't happen again. It's up to the two of you to determine whether this step of having an honest discussion of differences is necessary.

Step Five: Rebuild Respect

This last step is critical to making amends. Ask yourself what traits your friend possesses that inspire you to become a better person, and then make a list of a half dozen of your friend's most admirable qualities.

1. _____

   _____

2. _____

   _____

3. _____

   _____

4. _____

   _____

5. _____

   _____

6. _____

   _____

With this list completed, you are now ready to make amends. You will be able to express to your friend just how much you appreciate him or her based on these qualities.

relating to God
without feeling phony

Overview

In this session you will

- discuss your doubts and fears. Is it okay to doubt?
- discover how to really relate to God.
- hear some different conceptions of God.

Video:
Relating to God
Without Feeling Phony

Relating to God Relaxes Our Earthly Relationships

Curing Our Compulsion for Completion—Anne's Example

Doubt as Normal—Do I Have a Relationship with God?

Various Misconceptions of God—Referee, Grandfather, Scientist, Bodyguard

God as the Antidote for the Compulsion for Completion

On Your Own:
Honest-to-Goodness Doubt

How much do you struggle with doubt? The following continuums will help you consider your level of faith. Be as honest as you can in your responses.

My "faith" is nonexistent.   My faith is rock solid.

1   2   3   4   5   6   7   8   9   10

I don't know God.   I know God personally.

1   2   3   4   5   6   7   8   9   10

The Bible is just another book.   The Bible is a holy book
                                                  inspired by God.

1   2   3   4   5   6   7   8   9   10

Jesus was simply an historical figure.   Jesus is my personal Savior.

1   2   3   4   5   6   7   8   9   10

God doesn't hear my prayers.   God hears and answers my prayers.

1   2   3   4   5   6   7   8   9   10

As you consider where you stand on the above continuums, take a moment to summarize your faith in a single sentence.

_____

_____

Now take a moment to summarize your doubt in a single sentence.

_____

_____

Huddle Time:
Doubt's Place in Building Faith

In light of the exercise you just completed, discuss the following:

1. Does doubt have any place in an authentic relationship with God? Why or why not?
2. Do you believe God can help a person find a faith of his or her own? Explain.

Conference Call:
Misperceptions of God

- In the video, Leslie mentioned a few misperceptions people have about who God is. Do you identify with any of these? If so, how?

- If not, what misperception of God's character have you experienced?

On Your Own:
Does God Really Love Me?

This exercise is designed to help you assess the degree to which you experience God's love on a personal level. Rate each statement, using the scale below, to indicate how often each represents your beliefs. Take your time and be as honest as you can.

1—Rarely or never
2—A little of the time
3—Some of the time
4—A good part of the time
5—Most or all of the time

_____ I believe nothing could ever separate me from God's love.

_____ I accept how special I am to God.

_____ I believe God is love.

_____ God's grace permeates my life.

_____ I'm confident that because God loves me so much, he sacrificed his only Son in my place.

_____ I believe God loves me as if I were the only person on earth.

_____ I am free from irrational guilt feelings because of God's love.

_____ I believe I can do nothing to earn God's love because it's freely given.

_____ I know God loves me.

_____ I can love others because God first loved me.

Total score _____ x 2 = _____

Scoring: Add up your item scores and multiply your total by two. This provides a possible maximum score of 100. Use the following to interpret your score:

90–100 You have a solid and secure understanding of how much God loves you.

80–89 You may experience some ambivalence at times about how much God loves you, but deep down you rest in knowing that he does love you.

10–79 You are struggling to know whether God loves you or not. If your score is below 60, you would certainly benefit from counsel on God's grace.

Huddle Time:
Why We Need God

- If someone were to ask you why a person needs God, what would your answer be?

Extra-Mile Exercise

This final exercise may seem simple, but it is probably the most difficult one of all. It is designed to help you see how you relate to God now and how you want to relate to God in the future. It will help you formulate the steps necessary to develop your relationship with him.

In a single sentence, summarize your faith journey and how it has brought you to your present relationship with God. Then note a few key descriptors of your present relationship with him.

_____

_____

_____

Take a moment to consider how you might represent your present relationship with God by drawing a picture of it. Be as creative as you like. Use a separate piece of paper, if you wish.

Once you have completed your drawing, consider which aspects you would like to change to make it more like the relationship you long for. What would those changes involve?

_____

_____

_____

_____

What can you do, in practical terms, to make that kind of relationship with God a reality?

_____

_____

_____

_____

Love's Unseen Enemy

How to Overcome Guilt to Build Healthy Relationships

Dr. Les Parrott III

Too often efforts to build loving relationships are unwittingly sabotaged by an unseen enemy: guilt. In *Love's Unseen Enemy*, Dr. Les Parrott shows how to build healthier relationships by overcoming the feelings of false guilt and by dealing forthrightly with true guilt.

Dr. Parrott identifies the four relationship styles created by the combination of love and guilt:

- **Pleasers** love with their hearts, not their heads. They do loving things to relieve their guilt.
- **Controllers** can identify the problems with their minds, but don't always exude warmth and love.
- **Withholders** carry their guilt but are afraid to love.
- **Lovers** have learned to tap their capacity for genuine empathy. They strive to be loving, not simply to do loving things.

Parrott shows how your relational style affects your friendships, your marriage, your children, your work, and your relationship with God. Look for *Love's Unseen Enemy* at your local Christian bookstore.

Hardcover 0-310-40150-X
Mass Market Paperback 0-06-100940-7

ZondervanPublishingHouse

Grand Rapids, Michigan

http://www.zondervan.com

Becoming Soul Mates

52 Meditations to Bring Joy to Your Marriage

Les & Leslie Parrott

Becoming Soul Mates gives you a road map for cultivating rich spiritual intimacy in your relationship. Fifty-two practical weekly devotions help you and your partner dig deep for a strong spiritual foundation in the early years of marriage.

In each session you will find:

- An insightful devotion that focuses on marriage-related topics
- A key passage of Scripture
- Questions that will spark discussions on crucial issues
- Insights from real-life soul mates like Pat and Shirley Boone, Bill and Vonette Bright, and Norm and Joyce Wright
- Questions that will help you and your partner better understand each other's unique needs and remember them in prayer during the week.

Start building on the closeness you've got today and reap the rewards of a deep, more satisfying relationship in the years ahead. Pick up *Becoming Soul Mates* at your local Christian bookstore.

Hardcover 0-310-20014-8

ZondervanPublishingHouse

Grand Rapids, Michigan

http://www.zondervan.com

Getting Ready for the Wedding

All You Need to Know Before You Say I Do

Les and Leslie Parrott, General Editors

10 Topics the Wedding Consultant Can't Help You With

How do we know when we're ready for marriage? What's the secret to having a great engagement? How can we get married without drowning in debt?

Where better to turn for answers than to those who have gone before—experts in the areas of marriage, relationships, and finance, who know from experience what it takes to make the days leading up to the wedding (and the years that follow) a success!

The ten topics covered are:

- How to Know When You're Ready for Marriage (Les and Leslie Parrott)
- Secrets to Having a Great Engagement (David and Claudia Arp)
- Getting Married Without Drowning in Debt (Ron Blue)
- What to Do with Wedding Jitters (Robert and Rosemary Barnes)
- Making Your Wedding More Than a Ceremony (David and Jan Stoop)
- How to Have a Great Wedding Night (Clifford and Joyce Penner)
- Getting Married When Your Parents Don't Approve (John Trent)
- How to Handle the Wedding Bell Blues (H. Norman Wright)
- For Those Getting Married Again (Tom Whiteman)
- After the Honeymoon (Les and Leslie Parrott)

Softcover 0-310-21148-4

ZondervanPublishingHouse
Grand Rapids, Michigan
http://www.zondervan.com